I0022487

THE
LEGACY
JOURNAL

By: Precious Harrison-Cobb

Copyright © Precious Harrison-Cobb, 2020

All rights reserved. No part of this publication may be reproduced, distributed, or transmitted in any form or by any means, including photocopying, recording, or other electronic or mechanical methods, without prior written permission of the publisher and/or author, except that a reviewer may quote brief pages for review.

Disclaimer:

This book is not intended as a substitute for consultation with an attorney or any other professional. This book is designed to provide general information in regard to the subject matter covered. It is sold and published with the understanding that the publisher and/or author are not engaged in rendering legal or other professional services. For specific legal advice, you should consult with an attorney.

Every effort has been made to ensure that no copyrighted material has been used without permission. The author and/or publisher shall have neither liability nor responsibility to any person or entity with respect to any loss or damage that may result, or is alleged to result, directly or indirectly, by the information contained in this book.

ISBN: 978-1-7359096-0-8

Designed by: Adrian Aranas

To learn more about Attorney Precious Harrison-Cobb, go to **www.thelineagefirm.com**

"

The greatest disadvantage in life is living without a blueprint.

"

-Precious Harrison Cobb

In loving memory of

Isiah Harrison

Sarah Lenoir

JayCee Campbell

Ruby S. Harrison (Campbell)

Jackie Johnson

Lindy M. Harrison

Richard L. Archie

Yvonne Harrison Burton

Introduction

I've tried a number of ways to find an easy way of saying this. Truth is, there isn't one. DEATH IS REAL. Time and time again I've seen someone die unexpectedly or after a period of incapacity and his or her loved ones are left in chaos. Spending energy they don't have grieving and tirelessly working to get affairs in order.

Legacy has been defined as money or property left to one as an inheritance. It's also commonly known to be the story of a person that exists after death. In today's society we often attribute building a legacy to breaking generational curses or building generational wealth. The problem is that we work towards the idea of a legacy with little emphasis on planning for our absence.

It is this understanding that gave birth to this journal. It was through my own personal healing that I arrived at this place. I first encountered death at the age of eight. It was my grandfather and someone with a great presence in my life. As a child, you don't fully comprehend life and death as it is. But death greatly impacts a child's sense of security. My second eye opening experience was the death of my parents. My father, incarcerated before my birth and released when I was nine for only two years before he passed away. My mother raised me on her own with the support of her sisters and passed away when I was seventeen.

Through my healing I've taken inventory of how the loss I sustained has impacted my view on life and legacy. I understood that the challenges I faced weren't the result of the loss, but more about the type of legacy I was left with- those generational curses we were talking about.

As you work through this journal I will give you pieces of my experience and perspective to help you begin to craft your legacy. My hope is that you will use this journal to live more boldly. As an attorney, I know how important basic life and business planning can be. While this journal is not a substitute for legal advice, it should definitely inspire you to work towards a legacy that you can be proud of.

Table of Contents

What's Your Genesis?

Basic information tells us so much about a person and can be vital at the time of death or incapacity. The information in this section is commonly needed to complete a death certificate and is often unknown to others.

Name: .... *(First, Middle, Last)* AKA: ....

Gender: .... Race: .... DOB: .... Age: ....

SSN/Personal Identification #: ....

Birth Place

City: .... State: ....

Country: .... Citizenship: ....

Address

Street Name: ....

City: .... State: .... County: .... Zip: ....

Military Service (Armed Forces)

Branch: .... Retirement Status: .... Years in Service: ....

Marital Status

☐ Married ☐ Married, but separated ☐ Widowed ☐ Divorced ☐ Never Married

Spouse's Name: ....

Father

Father's Name: .... Father's DOB: .... Father's Birth City: ....

Mother

Mother's Name: .... Mother's DOB: .... Mother's Birth City: ....

Highest Education: ....

Occupation: ....

Who are you?

Our thoughts, beliefs, life experience, and interests help to define who we are. Take a moment to reflect on your life so that others don't define your legacy.

What are your life goals?

- 🌱 ....
....
....

- 🌱 ....
....
....
....

- 🌱 ....
....
....
....

- 🌱 ....
....
....
....

- 🌱 ....
....
....

- 🌱 ....
....
....

- 🌱 ....
....
....

- 🌱 ....
....
....

- 🌱 ....
....
....

- 🌱 ....
....
....

Most Important Life Lessons To-date

- 🌱
- 🌱
- 🌱
- 🌱
- 🌱
- 🌱
- 🌱
- 🌱
- 🌱
- 🌱

Most Memorable Experiences

🌱 ....
....
....

🌱 ....
....
....

🌱 ....
....
....

🌱 ....
....
....

🌱 ....
....
....

What do you enjoy doing with your time?

🌱 ....
....
....

🌱 ....
....
....

🌱 ....
....
....

🌱 ....
....

🌱 ....
....
....

What are your greatest accomplishments?

🌱 ....
....
....

🌱 ....
....
....

🌱 ....
....
....

🌱 ....
....
....

🌱 ....
....
....

Who or what has had the greatest influence on your life?

....
....
....
....
....
....
....
....
....
....
....
....

Worldviews/Beliefs

Key values/morals

Religious/Spiritual

Political

Social

Describe your...

Childhood

....
....
....
....
....
....
....
....

Teens

....
....
....
....
....
....
....
....

Adulthood

....
....
....
....
....
....
....
....

What are some challenges you've had to overcome?

Any regrets?

What keeps your family together?

What dreams do you have for your loved ones?

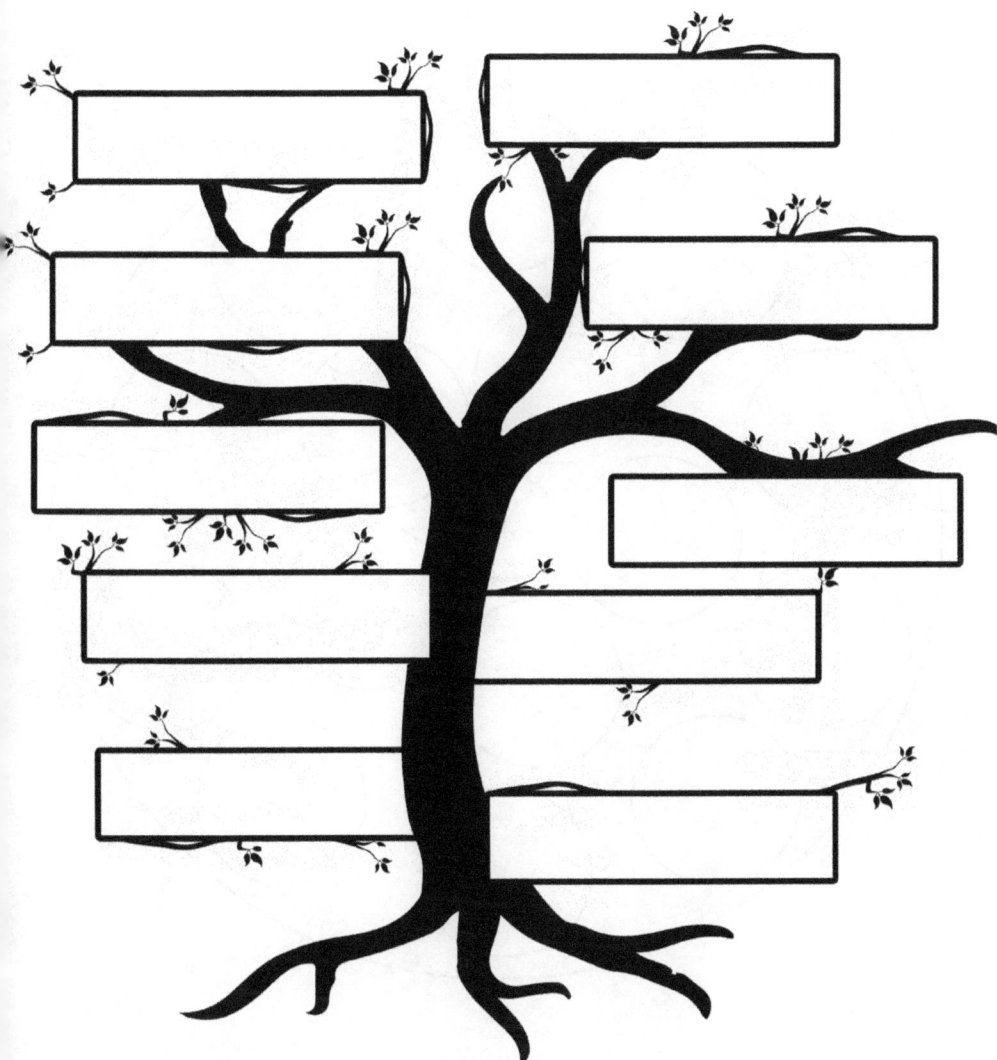

Family Tree

Friendship/ Support Circle

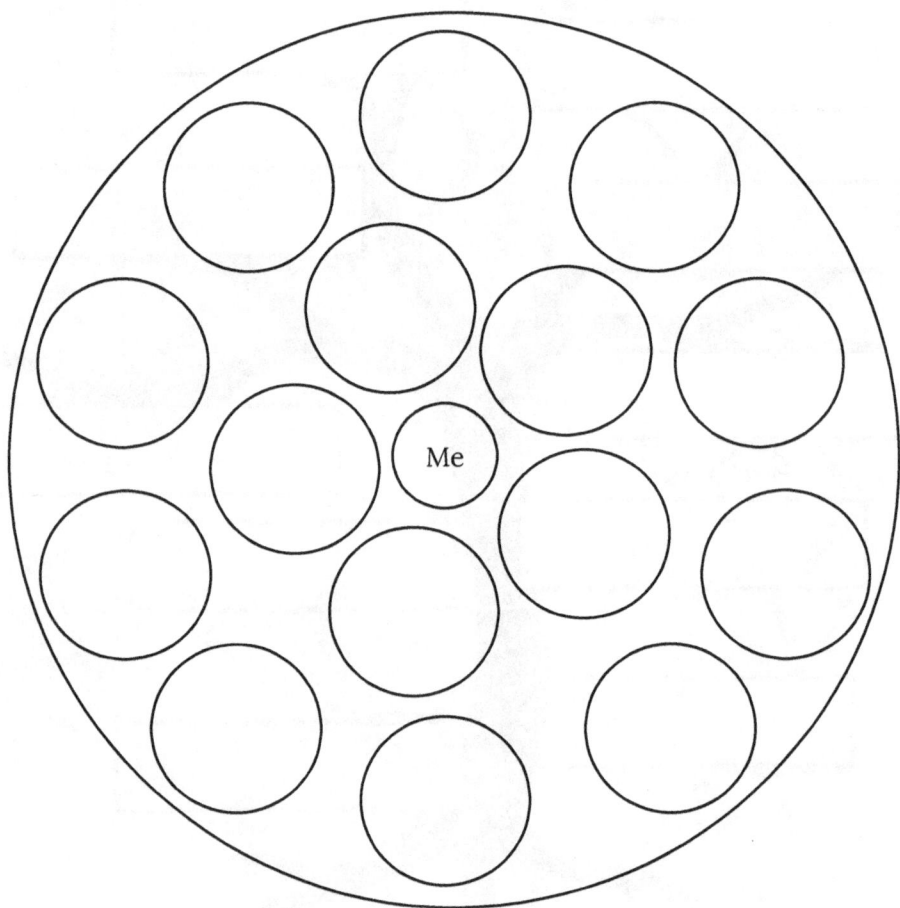

Me

Fruits of your labor

The fruits of your labor are proof of your existence. Taking the time to properly plan and identify your assets, liabilities, interests and investments can be crucial to your legacy. You secured the bag, now protect it.

Financial Assets

Assets	Institution	Account #	Owner	Balance /Contribution
Checking				
Checking				
Savings				
Savings				
Stocks/Bonds				
Stocks/Bonds				
Bitcoin/Digital Currency				
Bitcoin/Digital Currency				
529 Savings Plan				
529 Savings Plan				
401K				
Pension				

Sentimental Assets

Item/Description	Market Value	Location

Business Interests

Name of Business	Ownership Interest	Partners	Location of Incorporation

Intellectual Property Interests

Description	Legally Protected (Copyright, Trademark, Writers Guild of America etc.)	Date Created or Legally Protected	Location of Original

Financial Liabilities

Liabilities	Institution	Account #	Balance	Owner
Debt/Collection Account				
Debt/Collection Account				
Student Loan				
Vehicle Loan				
Home Mortgage				
Credit Card				
Credit Card				
Other				
Other				
Other				
Other				
Other				

General Expenses

Expenses	Provider	Amount	Payment Date	Co-Owners
Mortgage/Rent				
Homeowners/Renters Insurance				
HOA/Co-op				
Vehicle Payment				
Phone Bill				
Gas				
Electric				
Water				
Vehicle Insurance				
Health Insurance				
Pet Care				
Child Care				
Cable/Internet				
Video Streaming				
Music Streaming				
Credit Card				
Court Ordered Payments				

Social Media Assets

Platform	Name/Handle	Personal/Professional

Thinking ahead...

Legacy requires planning. Failure to plan is a disservice to you and the people you love. Taking the opportunity to plan for your healthcare, financial security and the care of others is crucial.

Medical

Insurance Provider: .... Account Number: ....

Primary Care Physician

Clinic Name: ....

Physician Name: .... Telephone: ....

Address: .... Email: ....

Medical Diagnosis: ....

Specialty Physician

Clinic Name: ....

Physician Name: .... Telephone: ....

Address: .... Email: ....

Do Not Resuscitate (DNR)

Location of Order: ....

Granting Physician: ....

Life Insurance

Company	Benefciary	Amount
....	....	....
....	....	....
....	....	....

Burial Arrangements

Funeral

Name: ....

Address: ....

Original Contract Location: .... Balance Due: ....

Burial Deed/Plot

Lot/Section: ....

Cemetery: .... Owner: ....

Original Deed Location: .... Balance Due: ....

Specific Wishes/Instructions:

Minor/Incapacitated Adult Guardianship

Name: ....

Child's DOB: .... Proposed Guardian: ....

Alternative Guardian: .... Special Needs: ....

Name: ....

Child's DOB: .... Proposed Guardian: ....

Alternative Guardian: .... Special Needs: ....

Name: ....

Child's DOB: .... Proposed Guardian: ....

Alternative Guardian: .... Special Needs: ....

Name: ....

Child's DOB: .... Proposed Guardian: ....

Alternative Guardian: .... Special Needs: ....

Name: ....

Child's DOB: .... Proposed Guardian: ....

Alternative Guardian: .... Special Needs: ....

Elder Care

Name: .... DOB: ....

Type of Guardianship (Legal/POA/None): ....

Proposed Guardian: .... Special Needs: ....

Name: .... DOB: ....

Type of Guardianship (Legal/POA/None): ....

Proposed Guardian: .... Special Needs: ....

Pet Care

Name: .... DOB: .... Veterinarian/Clinic: ....

Insurance: .... Special Needs: ....

Name: .... DOB: .... Veterinarian/Clinic: ....

Insurance: .... Special Needs: ....

Financial Planning

Accountant Name: .... Address: ....

Phone: .... Email: .... Personal/Business: ....

Accountant Name: .... Address: ....

Phone: .... Email: .... Personal/Business: ....

Estate Planning

Document	Date Created/ Modified	Drafted By (Attorney, Software, Handwritten-You etc.) Name, Address, Phone	Location of Original Document
Last Will and Testament	....	....	....
Financial Power of Attorney	....	....	....
Healthcare Power of Attorney	....	....	....
Advance Healthcare Directive-Living Will	....	....	....
Trust	....	....	....
Trust	....	....	....
Do not Resuscitate	....	....	....

It's your story, write it!

No legacy is the same but we all have the power to create our own.

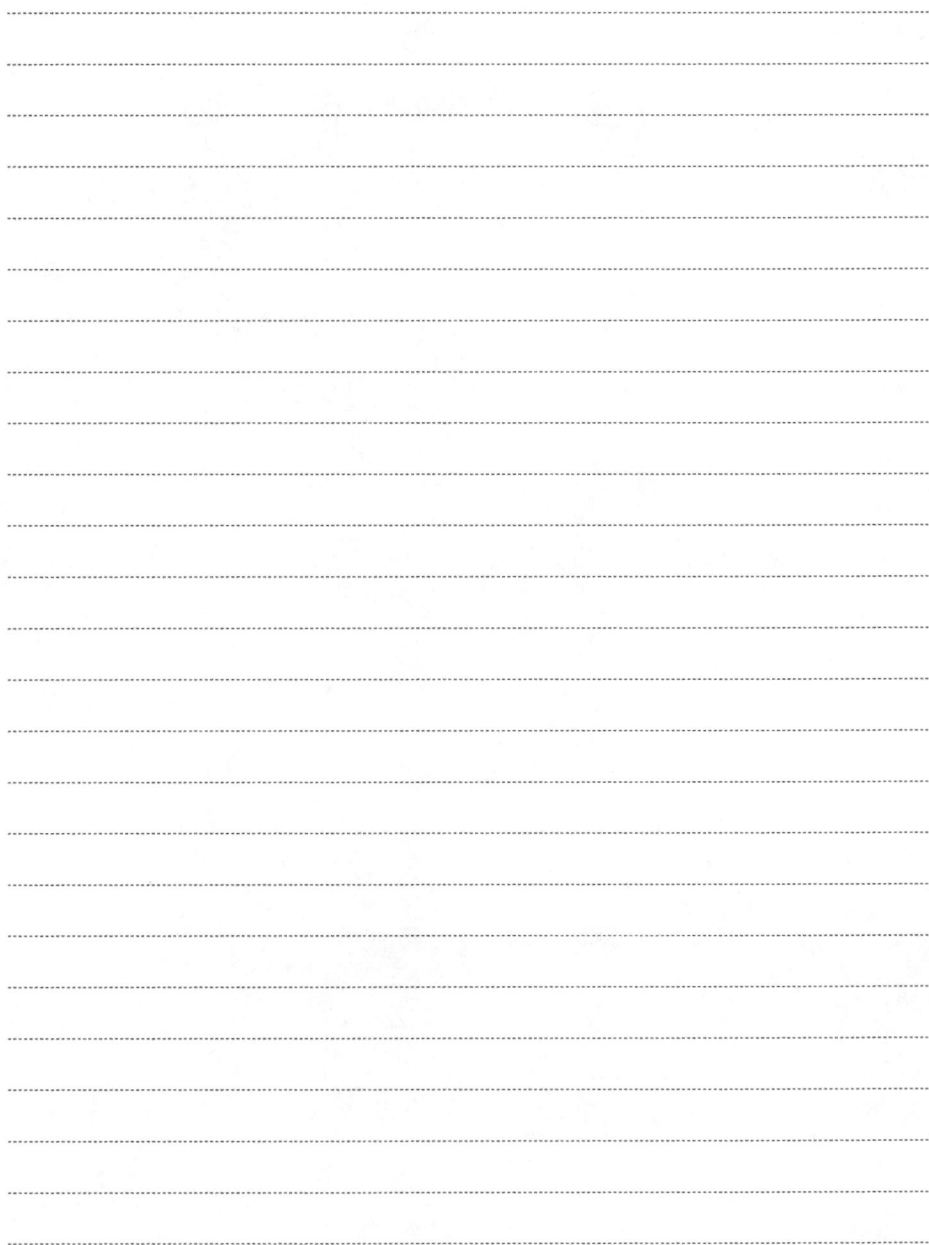

www.ingramcontent.com/pod-product-compliance
Lightning Source LLC
Chambersburg PA
CBHW021550270326
41930CB00008B/1446